A NOTE TO PARENTS FROM

Pat Boone

All children, even very small ones, love listening to stories from the Bible. And I love telling them. For years I've been sharing my favorites, first with my four daughters and now with all my grandchildren.

For this book, I've picked out nine best-loved stories from the Old Testament. I've set them down just the way I tell them when I've got one or more of my grandkids snuggled up on my lap. Of course, I've done a lot of "fiddling"—I've made the stories very simple and I've also tried hard to explain things in a very childlike way, a way that even a three-year-old will have no trouble understanding. That's why, for instance, I call God's new world a "big beautiful park," because the idea of paradise is a hard one to grasp, even for us grownups.

But what I have not changed—and what I hope comes through on every page—is the truth and spirit of the Bible and the wonderful message of God's never-ending love.

PAT BOONE'S Favorite
BIBLE STORIES
for the Very Young

ILLUSTRATED BY HANS WILHELM

RANDOM HOUSE ⌂ NEW YORK

"But watch out! Be very careful never to
forget what you've seen God doing for you.
May His miracles have a deep and permanent
effect upon your lives! Tell your children
and grandchildren about the glorious miracles
He did." (Deut. 4:9, Living Bible)

This book is dedicated to the parents and the grandparents who understand the timeless responsibility to teach their children about God from His own Holy Word—and who savor the priceless delight of that rich relationship.

This book is also dedicated to the fortunate children who hunger to know the good things, and the best.

Pat Boone

Text copyright © 1984 by Pat Boone. Illustrations copyright © 1984 by Hans Wilhelm. All rights reserved under International and Pan-American Copyright Conventions. Published in the United States by Random House, Inc., New York, and simultaneously in Canada by Random House of Canada Limited, Toronto.

Library of Congress Cataloging in Publication Data:
Boone, Pat. Pat Boone's Favorite Bible stories for the very young. SUMMARY: Includes the Creation, the Fall, Noah's Ark, the Tower of Babel, Samson and Delilah, and other stories. 1. Bible stories, English—O.T. [1. Bible stories—O.T.] I. Wilhelm, Hans, 1945– ill. II. Title. III. Title: Favorite Bible stories for the very young. BS551.2.B66 1984 221.9'505 84-6837 ISBN: 0-394-85891-3 (trade); 0-394-95891-8 (lib. bdg.)
Manufactured in the United States of America   1 2 3 4 5 6 7 8 9 0

CONTENTS

HOW THE WORLD BEGAN

How did the world begin? Well, I'm going to tell you. But first I want you to snuggle up and close your eyes real tight. That's right, no peeking. Now, see how dark it is? You can't see anything, can you? Try to imagine what it was like when there was no world. No sun in the sky. No stars or moon. No birds or animals. There weren't any people either—no Mommy, no Daddy, no you. Nobody anywhere!

But do you know who was there? God. God was there before any of these things. He can do anything, you know, and once He decided He wanted to make the world, He knew everything that it needed.

First He said to Himself, "It's too dark here. I can't see anything. I'd better have some light." And you know as soon as He said that, there was blazing, beautiful light everywhere. And He said, "Ahh, that's good. That's better. Now I can see." But He knew He needed to keep some darkness, too, so that kids could get to sleep at night. So He called the light "day," and the darkness He called "night." And He said, "That's a good arrangement. I'll keep it that way."

The next day He decided that He'd better create some water, because the world was nothing but a big dry ball of dirt. So God made oceans and rivers and lakes, and He set up a sprinkling system that He called rain. Now water could fall from the sky to the ground and make things grow. And God said, "Well, I think that's enough for one day. I'll take the rest of the day off." And He did.

The next day He looked at the ground and saw how bare it was. "I think I'll make grass," God said. "That would look nice." He made some trees, too, beautiful trees with leaves and fruit. And flowers. Yes, lots and lots of flowers. It took God all of the third day to make the world look like one great big beautiful park. But God still had a lot more work to do. So the next day God said, "Now I'll make a great big sun in the sky to keep the world warm and bright. And even at night, when it's dark, I'll have a little light." So God made the moon and the stars. He did all that on the fourth day.

And after He put the sun, the moon, and the stars in the sky, He said, "That was a pretty good job. I like that."

The next day, when God looked at the oceans and the rivers and the lakes and the ponds, He said, "I know what that water needs. It needs fish!" And right then and there He created all kinds of fish—big fish, little fish, fancy fish in every color of the rainbow, plain fish that are good to eat, and even some fish that eat other fish. God was happy to see all the fish swimming in the water. "But now the sky looks so empty," He said. So God created birds—all the birds you've ever seen and lots more that you've probably never seen.

God made them all. And He said, "Those birds and fish will make other birds and fish, just like themselves. I've done a good day's work." And that was the end of the fifth day.

Well, the next day God looked around at the grass and the flowers and the fish and the birds and He thought, "There's something else the world needs . . . animals! That's what the world needs. I'll make all kinds. They can eat the grass and other plants and grow big and strong." And so He made cows and He made horses and He made elephants and He made—well, can you guess what else He made? How about something that goes "woof!" And something that goes "meowww!" Yes, that's right. He made dogs and cats. And mice and moose. And lions and tigers and other ferocious animals. And He made some funny animals too. Like anteaters and hippos and skunks. Yes, God thought it would be very funny if there was a little black and white animal that sprayed you with a *horrible* smell if you got too close and made it mad.

Making all those animals. What a lot of work that was! But even after all that, God felt there was still something missing. He thought a minute. And then He knew what the world needed most of all. Can you guess?

Did you say people? Yes. You are absolutely right. He wanted people, people He could talk to and who could enjoy the wonderful world He'd made. And so toward the end of that sixth day He created a man.

How did He do it? Well, He took some dirt in his hands and He packed it and rolled it around and shaped it until He had made a man—a man who looked, well, a little like God. But the man couldn't move. He couldn't think. He was just like a doll. So then God put His face very close to the man's face and He breathed into the man's nose. And do you know what? The man began to wiggle and his eyes popped open and he looked right into the face of God. And he said, "Hi, God. Are you my daddy?"

And God said, "Yes, I am. And you are my son. You're a living man now and I'm going to call you Adam."

And do you know who else God made? A woman, that's who! God said, "Adam, you're going to take a nap now." Then He put Adam to sleep, and while Adam was asleep God took out one of his ribs. It didn't hurt at all. Really. God can do things like that. He just took out one of Adam's ribs and He went to work on that rib until He made another person. She was a lot like Adam, except she was a woman. Then God breathed life into her and she said, "Hi, Daddy!" And God decided to call her Eve because that name means the mother of all living things. "Eve, take a look at this man," God told her, and Eve did. "Ooh, I like him," she said. "Can we be friends?" And God said yes because that was just what He wanted.

So God woke Adam up and introduced him to Eve.

"Adam and Eve," God said to His children, "look at this huge, beautiful park—this great big world—I've made for you. Do you like it?"

Adam and Eve said, "Oh, yes, we do. Thank you, Father. Thank you, God."

God liked hearing that. It made Him so happy, He said, "Everything else that I've created—all the plants, all the birds, all the fish, all the animals—I'm giving them to you. They're for your pleasure, for you to have fun with. They'll be your friends. But I'll be your best friend. And I'll come visit you every day. And we'll all live happily ever after. Okay?" And Adam and Eve said, "Okay! That's great!"

And so the end of the sixth day came and not only did God rest that night but all the next day too, because you have to agree that making all of those things was a lot of work for God.

It was a good world. And God made a good man and a good woman to live in it. But did they live happily ever after, the way God meant them to? No, they didn't. I know you must be wondering why. But that's another story.

THE GARDEN OF EDEN

Time to hop back on my lap again! I'm going to tell you the rest of the story about Adam and Eve.

Well, for a long, long time they lived in a special park that God had made for them. It was called the Garden of Eden. They had so much fun there, just like God wanted them to. Their favorite game was thinking up names for all the animals.

Adam would say, "Oh, look, Eve. Here comes a tall animal with a long neck and spots on it. I think I'll call it a giraffe. Yes, that's a good name for it."

And then Eve would say, "Adam, see that nice fat animal over there? The one that goes 'mooo' and has a tail that can swat you in the face if you don't watch out. Well, I'm going to name it a—"

Cow! Did you say a cow? Why, that's just what Eve called it too!

Of course, Adam and Eve didn't spend all their time playing this game. Sometimes they went swimming. Sometimes they had picnics. You know, the Garden of Eden had everything good that you like to eat. It was all right there. And if Adam and Eve wanted some milk, they'd just say, "Cow, come here. We'd like some milk, please." And the cow would say, "Mooo, okay. Have all you want. Just leave enough for my little calf."

God liked visiting Adam and Eve very much. He showed them how to plant things and how to fish and He even taught them how to sing.

God taught them so many things. Now, one thing God wanted to teach Adam and Eve was to obey Him, to mind what He said. So He gave them one order. Only one little order. He said, "You see that big tree over there in the middle of the garden?

I don't want you to eat any of its fruit. Not ever ever ever. That's the Tree of the Knowledge of Good and Evil, and if you eat any of its fruit, you'll have to leave the Garden of Eden. You'll have to go far away from me, and one day you'll die. And I don't want that to happen. So don't eat any of that fruit. Promise?"

Adam and Eve nodded. "We promise, Daddy," they said.

For a long time they listened to what God had told them, and they stayed away from that special tree.

But one day this long, long skinny creature came along. He had smooth scales all over him and a little tongue that went click-click—a little tongue that just darted in and out so fast you could hardly see it. What do you think this creature was called?

A snake! Yes. Adam and Eve called him a snake. They liked that snake. He was smart and fun to be around and he always seemed to say just what you wanted to hear.

One day the snake said to Eve, "You're not going to believe all that stuff God said, are you? All that stuff about never eating any fruit from that special tree, that pretty tree with all that yummy fruit on it?"

And Eve said, "But God told us we'll die if we eat that fruit."

The snake slithered up to the special tree and poked his head through the branches. "Die? What does that mean?" the snake asked Eve.

Eve thought about that. "I don't know," she said. "But it sounds bad."

Right away the snake said, "Don't you see? God is just trying to scare you. I'll tell you why He doesn't want you to eat that fruit. Because if you do, you'll be as smart as He is. And God doesn't want that. Oh, no! He wants to be smarter than everybody else."

Eve said, "Do you really think so? But my daddy has always told me the truth . . ."

"Trust me," hissed the snake. "Eat that fruit, just a little bitty piece. Then see how smart you'll be."

And then what do you think? Eve went right over and picked a piece of that fruit and ate some. Now, Adam should have been saying to Eve, "Don't do that! Daddy told us not to!" But he just sat there and watched her. When nothing bad happened to Eve and she said, "Mmmm, this fruit *is* good," Adam said, "Hey, maybe I'll try some too!" And he did.

But do you know what? The snake had tricked them. The fruit did not make Adam and Eve any smarter. What it did do was make them think mean things. Mean things they shouldn't say and mean things they shouldn't do.

Then suddenly the ground started trembling from the footsteps of God. He was looking for Adam and Eve. But they did not want to see Him. They were scared because they had disobeyed God, so they ran away and hid.

"Adam! Eve! Where are you?" God called out.

When He found them behind some bushes, He said, "What's the matter? Why are you hiding from me?"

Adam said, "I heard your voice. It frightened me."

"But why?" asked God. "I've never hurt you, have I?"

"No, well—well—I guess maybe we hid because Eve and I don't have any clothes on," Adam said.

But God said, "What difference does that make? You never had any clothes on before." Then He looked at Adam and Eve. He looked them right in the eye. "Did you eat any of the fruit from that tree?" He asked.

Now, of course, God already knew the answer was yes. How did He know that? Well, for one thing, God knows everything. And also He could tell that Adam and Eve were not feeling close to Him anymore. So He knew they must have eaten a piece of that fruit.

"Oh, Adam! Oh, Eve! Why did you do that?" God asked. He was so, so disappointed.

Adam and Eve hung their heads in shame. Then Eve said, "The snake talked me into it. The snake said eating the fruit would make me as smart as you."

Well, first God spoke to the snake. "Come here," He said. "You talked Adam and Eve into doing something very, very bad, something I told them not to do. So I'm going to make your life very hard. From now on, you won't have any friends on this earth. Not even one. People will run away from you. Sometimes they'll step on you and hurt you. And sometimes you will bite them and hurt them back. I'm sorry this is the way it has to be. But it's your fault, Snake."

Then God turned to Adam and Eve. They had never seen Him look so sad. "I love you both so much," He told them. "But you disobeyed me, so you have to leave the garden. Right now. And you can't come back. Not ever. From now on, life won't be easy, the way it's been here. You'll have to work hard. There will be times when the sun and the water won't be your friends—plants won't grow and you won't have enough to eat. It will not always be warm and pleasant. Sometimes you'll be very cold. And you'll be scared. All because you didn't listen."

Adam and Eve started to cry. And God felt so sorry for them that He gave them some clothes made of animal skins to keep them warm in winter.

Then God told two angels to stand at the entrance to the garden. As Adam and Eve walked out God said to the angels, "You can't let them back into the garden."

Adam and Eve were very scared now. And God said, "I'm sorry but it's true. And someday you are going to die. Someday you will lie down and go to sleep and you won't wake up again."

So Adam and Eve left the garden. And for the rest of their lives, they had to work very hard, just the way God said.

But do you know what? God never stopped loving Adam and Eve, even though they hadn't minded Him. He went right on loving them. And He went right on loving their children. And their children's children. And soon God had a whole lot of people to love. Including somebody who I think is very, very special. Do you know who that person is?

Why, you guessed it. It's you!

NOAH'S ARK

Do you like to take your bath at night? I thought so! I just knew you liked to splash around in the warm water and play with your little animals that float. Well, the next time you're in the tub having fun, maybe you'll think about Noah and the ark. Because this is a story about water. Lots and lots of water. And animals—all kinds of animals.

Now, let's see. Where did the last story end? Oh, yes! Adam and Eve had left the Garden of Eden and as time went by the world became full of people. And as more time went by the people became very wicked. They forgot all about God. They forgot about being kind and loving each other. All except Noah and his family.

One day God said to Himself, "The world has turned into such a bad place that I'm going to have to start all over again. I am going to send down rain. It's going to rain like it's never rained before. And all this rain is going to flood the earth and destroy everything on it. The only people I'm going to save are Noah and his wife and their sons and their wives. So when I start the world all over again, I'll start with them. With Noah and his family."

God saw Noah working in the fields and He told him that there would be a great flood. So He told Noah to build an ark. Do you know what an ark is? It's a great big boat. God said this great big boat had to be 450 feet long—that's even longer than a football field. And it had to be 75 feet wide, wider than a superhighway. And the ark had to be 45 feet high, as high as a three-story building. "The ark must also have three decks," God told Noah. "A top, a middle, and a bottom deck. And please don't forget to put a door on the side."

Now, perhaps you're wondering why the ark had to be so big if it was just for Noah and his family. Well, the answer is simple. It wasn't just for Noah and his family. Can you guess who else was going to live inside the ark?

Animals! Yes. That's right. Because when the world began again, there couldn't be just people. There had to be animals, too.

God told Noah, "I want you to go out and find two of every kind of animal—a boy and a girl of every animal on earth—from the biggest elephants to the teeny-tiniest ladybugs. And then I want you to take all those animals inside the ark with you and your family. You'll have to take lots of food along with you too. And as soon as the rain starts, you close that door. The rains are going to keep on coming down and pretty soon there's going to be so much water that the ark will float away with you and all those animals on it. Do you understand, Noah?"

Noah nodded.

"And you will do everything that I have said?" God asked.

"Yes, God, I will," Noah answered.

And he did. Noah did everything just the way God told him to.

It took him many years to build that big ark, because he and his family had to build it all by themselves. Nobody else would help. All the other people laughed and said, "You're crazy, Noah. It's not going to rain like you say. There is no God and there is not going to be any big flood."

But did Noah listen to them? No, of course not. And after the ark was finished, he and his family went out into the fields and forests, the mountains and rivers, and they found two of every single creature that lives on earth and they led them into the ark, two by two. And just when the very last animals were inside and Noah had shut the door, do you know what happened?

It started to rain.

Yes. It rained and it rained and it rained. For forty days and forty nights it kept right on raining. Soon the tallest trees were under water and then even the highest mountains were covered by the flood. All that was left was that great big ark bobbing and floating there on top of the waves with the rain coming down on it. And the only living things in the whole wide world were Noah and his family and all those animals.

Can you imagine what it was like inside that boat all that time with birds flying around and animals mooing and roaring and squealing and braying? What a lot of noise! Why, it was exactly like living in a zoo.

Even after the rain stopped, it was a long time before the water started to come down off the mountains and soak into the ground. Months and months went by. Then one day the ark finally came to rest on top of a mountain. A mountain called Ararat. But still, when Noah opened a window in the ark and looked out, all he could see was water. Water everywhere. It was just like being in the middle of the ocean. So he sent out a dove to look for land. But the dove flew right back because she couldn't find a tree anywhere to build a new nest.

After seven days Noah decided to send the dove out again. And do you know what? She came back that evening with an olive leaf in her beak. Now that meant there had to be trees and dry land somewhere nearby.

So a few days later Noah sent the dove out once more. And this time she didn't come back. Noah knew the dove had found a new home!

At last Noah and his family came out of the ark, and I'll bet they were so glad. They had been living on it for a whole year. Now they were ready to start a brand-new world. They let all the animals go. The animals ran and flew and crawled away. They made new homes for themselves, and Noah and his wife and children made a new home for themselves too.

God was happy that all the animals had been saved and He was happy that there were good people on the earth who believed in Him.

"I will never send another flood like that again," God promised Noah. "I will never curse the earth and destroy all living things. Never again. And as a sign of my promise, I'm putting a rainbow up here in the sky. That's my signature. It's my name in bright, beautiful colors."

And now, every time it rains and people become scared that maybe there's going to be another great flood, they can look into the sky and see a rainbow. And they can remember God's promise that the earth will never be destroyed by a flood again.

And you know it never has, and it never will.

THE TOWER OF BABEL

Well, you know what happened after the flood, don't you? The world started up again. That's right. And pretty soon there were lots of people again. Thousands of them. They built a city called Babel and they all lived together like one big family.

Everybody had heard the story of Adam and Eve and how they had once lived in a wonderful place called the Garden of Eden where God came to visit them. Of course, they knew nobody could ever go back to that garden, but they believed they could make their own special place, maybe even better than the Garden of Eden! After all, there were so many of them now. They could do anything they wanted to, couldn't they?

So do you know what the people of Babel decided to do? They decided to build a giant tower. They were going to make that tower so high that it would reach right up into heaven! That sure would be special! That would prove that they were special just like Adam and Eve.

Now, you might think that sounds impossible. But it wasn't. Because God made people very smart and very strong. So they started to work on that giant tower. They built it out of bricks. Lots and lots of bricks. Everybody helped each other. If a person shouted "I need more bricks!" somebody would bring a bucketful right away. And pretty soon the tower of Babel was higher even than the Empire State Building. And still the people kept on working.

Well, God saw what was happening. He looked down from heaven and He said to the angels, "Just look at what my children are doing. Look at that tower. It's getting higher every day. They sure are smart and hardworking. But I wish they had asked my advice before they started doing that."

Now, God loved His children and wanted them to be with Him in heaven. But *He* had to decide when it was the right time for them to get there. And it wasn't the right time yet, because the people were doing things they wanted to do, instead of asking God what He wanted. Just like Adam and Eve.

So God said to the angels, "I must stop my children. And I know just how to do it. The people of Babel all speak the same language now. When someone says something, everybody else understands what he means. But if I give them all different languages, no one will know what anybody else is saying. And they won't be able to finish that tower."

And that's just what happened.

All of a sudden, a person working up on a ladder said, "Excuse me, you down there. Could you hold on to my ladder so I won't fall?"

But to the person below, the question came out sounding like "Ishkabibblefribble." So he answered, "What are you talking about? I don't understand what you want me to do." And *his* words sounded just like nonsense to the person up on the ladder. It sounded like "Kammaframmanapolis."

And so because nobody could understand anybody else, the people of Babel couldn't work together or help each other anymore. So they put down their tools and they came down from the tower. And finally the big unfinished tower fell down into a pile of dust and broken bricks.

As for the people, they all went their separate ways. All over the world. And that's why there are so many different languages in the world today. Chinese and German and Swahili and Hindustani and Hebrew and English and French and Spanish and so many more. All because the people of Babel wanted to do what they thought was "special"—instead of talking to God and finding out what He wanted.

That's too bad, because only God knows what's really special. Aren't you glad that God wants us to talk to Him and that He understands every language?

JOSEPH AND HIS BROTHERS

So far the Bible stories I've told you have been about grownups, haven't they? Well, now I'm going to tell you a story about a little boy. At least, he was a little boy at the start of the story.

This little boy was named Joseph. And he had eleven brothers. That's a big family, isn't it! Their father was named Jacob, and Jacob always loved Joseph just a little more than his other children. Maybe it was because Joseph was such a good little boy. Or maybe it was because Joseph was born when Jacob was quite an old man. Anyway, that's the way it was. The other brothers all knew Joseph was their father's favorite, and they didn't like it. Joseph got to stay at home while they had to work in the fields. And he was given a special coat to wear—a beautiful coat of many different colors. This made his brothers jealous. Very jealous indeed.

One day Joseph decided to go out in the fields to visit his big brothers. He was wearing his special coat, the one his father had given him. So anybody could tell it was Joseph, even from far away. And when his brothers saw him coming, a couple of them said, "There's that spoiled brat brother of ours. The one our father loves so much. When he gets here, let's kill him! Let's throw him down in a deep pit with no food and leave him there to die!"

What a terrible thing to think of doing to anybody, but especially their own little brother! But they meant it. They said, "We can tell our father that a wild animal came and ate Joseph up. And he'll never know what really happened."

Well, Ruben, who was the oldest, knew how wrong that would be. But he pretended to go along with his brothers. "All right," he said. "Let's throw him in the pit. That's a good way to get rid of him." But all along he had an idea of how to save Joseph.

32

Just then Joseph arrived. He waved and said hi to all his brothers. And do you know what they did? They grabbed him and tore off his coat and then they threw Joseph down into the pit. He must have been a scared little boy.

Ruben sneaked off while all this was going on. He went to find some food for Joseph. You see, he figured he'd come back for his little brother that night and bring him home, safe and sound.

Now, that was a pretty good plan Ruben had to save his brother. But it just didn't work out that way. Oh, no. Because while Ruben was gone, a band of traders came by. They were traveling all the way to Egypt.

When the brothers saw them, one of them shouted, "Hey, I've got a great idea. Let's sell Joseph to these traders. We'll get some money, and that's better than just killing him. Besides, he'll be far off in Egypt. And we won't ever have to see him again. Ever."

So that's just what they did.

And after Joseph was taken away by the traders, his brothers took his coat and smeared it with the blood of a dead goat. Then they went running back to their father's house.

"Look! Look at Joseph's coat!" they cried. "A lion or some wild animal must have killed him and eaten him up. All that's left is his coat!"

When Jacob heard this, he fell down and cried. He cried for weeks. Yes, he did. Over and over he kept on saying, "Oh, my son, my son Joseph is dead and I will never see him again."

Now, I bet you're thinking, "Poor Jacob. What a sad story this is." But you know what? The story doesn't end here. Oh, no, there's a lot more. You see, when Joseph got to Egypt, first he became the servant of a wealthy man. And then he became the servant of the king of Egypt. Joseph worked so hard and did so many favors for that king that soon he became very rich and powerful. Almost a king himself.

One night the king had a very strange dream. He dreamed that seven fat cows were eating some grass in a meadow. Then seven skinny cows came along and ate up the fat cows.

The king woke up with a start. He sure was glad that scary dream was over. The next morning he asked Joseph what he thought the dream meant.

"I think God is showing you what is going to happen," Joseph said. "The seven fat cows mean that for the next seven years there will be good crops and lots of food for everybody. But the seven skinny cows mean that for seven years after that, there won't be enough food. People will be hungry all across the land."

"You really think that's what my dream was about?" said the king.

"Yes," said Joseph, "and we'd better get ready for all those years when there isn't going to be any food. We'd better get started right now, storing up lots of fruits and vegetables and meat, so that when the seven good years are over and the seven bad years come, the people of Egypt won't have to go hungry."

So that's just what they did. And do you know, the king's dream did come true. For seven years there were good harvests and plenty to eat. But after that the crops suddenly began to die. Not just in Egypt. All over the world. But in Egypt people didn't have to go hungry because of all the food Joseph had saved up.

Now, by this time Joseph's father, Jacob, was a very old man. And he was very worried because his family had nothing to eat. He had heard there was food in Egypt, so he sent his sons there to try and get some.

Just as soon as the brothers got to Egypt, they went to see a man they'd heard about. A man who was very rich and powerful. Almost a king himself. They begged him for food. "It is not just for ourselves," they said. "But for our father, who is very old and weak now."

Well, when the man heard this, he began to cry. And, of course, you know why. Because that man was Joseph. Yes, that's right!

He hugged the men and said, "I am your brother Joseph. You sold me to the traders. You thought you would never see me again and I thought I would never see you again. But here we are!" Joseph saw how scared his brothers looked now. They knew how rich and powerful he was. He could have *them* killed if he wanted to! "Don't be afraid," he said, hugging all his brothers. "All these years God has been watching over me. Just as He has been watching over you. I will not harm you. I want to help. I will give you all the food you need. All I ask is that you bring my father here so that we can all live together. One big family again."

And so that's just what they did, for many, many years. You see? The story does have a happy ending. You just had to wait a little while to get to it.

SAMSON AND DELILAH

Can you show me how to make a muscle? That's right. You certainly are getting big and strong.

Did you know there's a story in the Bible about someone who was very, very strong? His name was Samson. He lived a very long time ago in the land of Israel.

When Samson was just a little baby, his mother promised God that she would never cut Samson's hair. And you know, she never did. She never let him go to a barber shop. She never trimmed his hair, even a little. In return God made Samson strong. Stronger than anybody else in the world.

When Samson grew up, his mother told him about the promise she'd made. "You must keep the promise too," she said to her son.

"I will," Samson said. "I will never cut my hair. And I won't ever tell anybody that my long hair is part of my promise to God, and that's why I'm so strong."

Now, I bet you're wondering just how strong Samson was. Well, one time a lion sprang out of some bushes and jumped on Samson. Samson didn't have a gun or even a knife. All he did was grab that lion by its jaws and tear it apart. Just like a piece of paper. That's how strong Samson was!

Samson was brave, too. He wasn't at all afraid of the Philistines. The Philistines didn't believe in God. And they wanted to make all the people of Israel their slaves.

One day the Philistines found out Samson was in a cave. I'm really not sure what he was doing in that cave. Maybe he was camping out there. Well, three thousand Philistine soldiers came to get Samson, to take him out of that cave and make him their prisoner. Now, Samson wasn't going to let that happen. So he ran out of that cave, picked up a big bone that was lying on the ground, and killed a thousand Philistine soldiers! The rest of them got so scared, they ran away as fast as they could.

Well, of course, after this all the Philistines were afraid of Samson. And they all wanted to find out what made him so strong. But they figured Samson wasn't ever going to tell them. And they were right.

But then one day Samson fell in love with a woman named Delilah. She was young. And she was beautiful. And she was a Philistine.

Samson knew Delilah should not be his sweetheart, because her people were the enemies of his people, the people of Israel. But he loved her very much and he thought he could trust her.

Poor Samson. Was he wrong!

The Philistines came to Delilah and they said, "If you find out what makes Samson so strong, we'll give you lots of money."

And Delilah said, "Okay, I'll do my best."

So every day Delilah kept asking Samson, "Why are you so strong? You can tell me. I won't tell anybody else. Trust me."

Samson knew he wasn't supposed to tell anybody about his hair. So he told Delilah a fib. He said, "If anybody ties me up with a leather rope, I'll become weak. I'll be just like any other man."

"Oh, so that's it," Delilah said. Then she waited for Samson to take a nap and the minute he was asleep, she got a leather rope and tied Samson up with it. Then she called in some of her Philistine soldier friends to take Samson off to jail. But when they got to Samson's house, Samson woke up and he snapped that leather rope right off. Just as if it were a piece of thread. And all the Philistine soldiers ran away as fast as they could.

A few days later Delilah started in again, asking Samson, "What is the secret of your strength, Samson? Come on, you can tell me. I'm your sweetheart, aren't I?"

Now, Samson didn't realize it was Delilah who tricked him before, and he still loved her very much. But he remembered that he wasn't ever supposed to tell about his hair, so he made up another fib. He said, "If you tie me up with a brand-new rope, one that's never been used before, then I won't be strong anymore."

I bet you know what happened next, don't you? As soon as Samson lay down to take a nap, Delilah got out a brand-new rope and tied it around and around Samson. "Samson is your prisoner now!" she shouted to the Philistine soldiers, and they came racing in again, all ready to take him away. Well, that's when Samson woke up. And he snapped that new rope right off. Just as if it were a piece of ribbon. And all the Philistine soldiers had to run away again.

Right away Delilah started crying. "Samson, you don't love me," she said, and then sobbed some more. "Because if you did, you'd tell me the truth. You'd tell me what makes you so strong."

Samson was so tired of her begging and her crying that he said, "All right, I'll tell you. It's my hair. It has grown since I was a little baby because my mother made a promise to God that it would never be cut. And if it ever is cut, why, then I won't be strong anymore."

So the very next time Samson went to sleep, Delilah got out some scissors and—snip! snip! snip!—she cut off Samson's hair until it was even shorter than yours. And this time, when the Philistine soldiers came for Samson, he couldn't even put up a little fight. He was *that* weak.

Well, the Philistines took Samson off to jail. They put out his eyes and made him blind. They made him their slave and gave him lots of hard work to do. And they made fun of Samson too. "You're not so tough now, are you?" the Philistine soldiers would say, and then laugh.

But you know, there was one thing the Philistines did not notice the whole time they were teasing Samson and making his life so miserable. Can you guess what it was?

His hair had begun to grow again! Yes. It grew and grew until it was very long. Then Samson prayed to God. "God, I know I was wrong," Samson said. "I'm sorry. I never should have told anybody where my strength came from. I should never have broken my promise to you. But now my hair is long again, and I pray that you will give me one more chance to destroy the enemies of Israel."

Not long after that, the Philistines decided to have a tremendous party in a great hall—their big convention center. Thousands of people came. Samson was brought out before all the guests so they could laugh at him. And while everyone was eating and drinking and laughing, Samson prayed once again.

"Oh, dear God," he said, "please give me my strength again. Right now."

And then Samson took hold of two giant columns, the two main posts that held up the roof of the hall. And he pulled and he pulled and he pulled until—CRASH!—down fell the columns and down fell the roof on top of all those people.

Everybody was killed. Samson too. But God had answered his prayer. He gave Samson his strength back. And He let him destroy the enemies of Israel.

Isn't it too bad that this big strong man didn't keep his promise to God? What good are muscles if you don't use them for the right things?

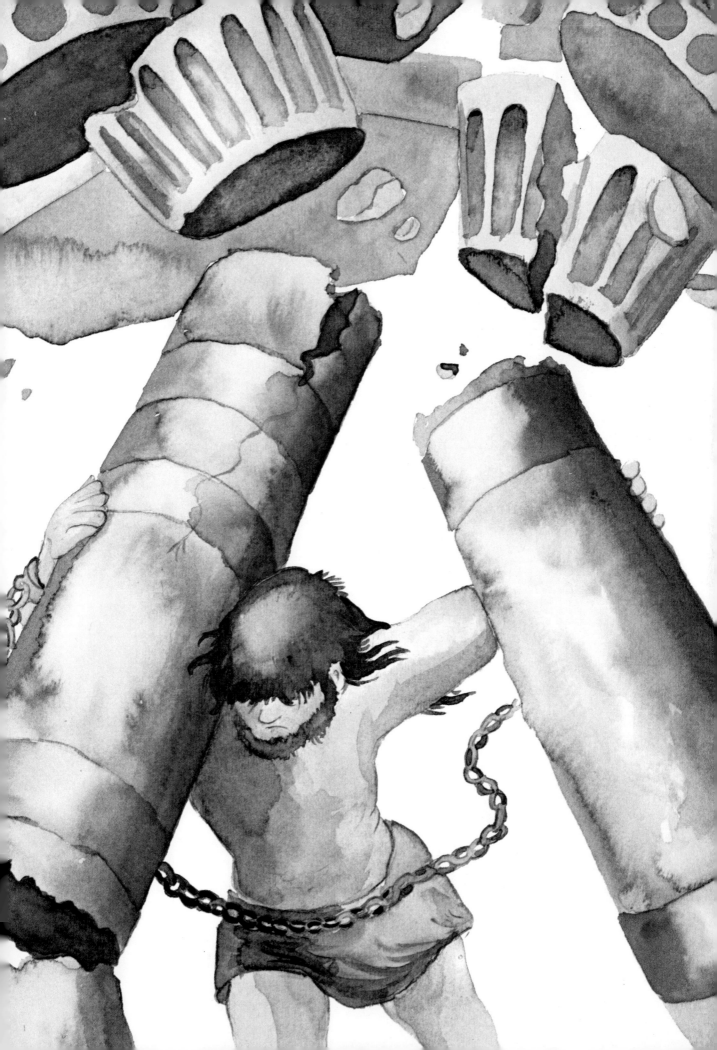

DAVID AND GOLIATH

Do you think giants are only in fairy tales? Well, they aren't. There's a story in the Bible about a giant—a giant named Goliath— and the boy who fought him. The boy's name was David.

David was a shepherd boy. But he wanted to be a soldier. All his brothers were in the army of Israel. They had all gone off to fight the Philistines, the enemies of Israel. But David was too young. He had to stay at home and look after his father's sheep.

David missed his brothers, so one day he decided to go visit them. He walked and he walked until he came to a hill. All the soldiers in the army of Israel had camped out there. And not too far away, on top of another hill, David could see the Philistine army. Thousands of Philistine soldiers.

But there was no fighting going on. David couldn't figure out why. Then he looked down in the valley, between the two hills. There stood the biggest man David had ever seen in his whole life. Can you guess who it was?

Goliath! That's right. He was more than ten feet tall. There was heavy armor on his chest and legs. And he carried a big sword and a spear.

"Why don't you men of Israel send out some soldier to fight me?" Goliath shouted. "If he beats me in battle, then I and all the rest of the Philistines will be the slaves of the people of Israel. The war will be over. But if *I* win, then all the soldiers of Israel will become our slaves. Now send out one of your soldiers and let's settle this."

But, of course, none of the Israeli soldiers wanted to go fight this giant. Even the king was afraid. But not David. He went to the king and said, "Let me fight Goliath."

The king looked at David and said, "Don't be silly. You're just a young boy. How could you ever win against that giant? Now go away. Don't bother me. We have problems here."

"Please give me a chance," David said. "When I'm taking care of my father's sheep, sometimes a lion will come and try to steal one of them. But I know God is right there to help me. So I just hit the lion over the head with a club and kill him. And if a bear tries to take away one of our sheep, I do the same thing to that bear. I'm not afraid of lions or bears. And I'm not afraid of that giant, either. God will help me."

Well, after hearing this brave young boy, the king changed his mind. He said, "All right. You go and fight Goliath. And God be with you." The king tried to give David his armor—his helmet and his chestplate and the pieces that went on his arms and legs. But they were too big and too heavy for David.

"I can't fight with all this on," David told him. "I didn't have any armor when I fought the lions and the bears. All I need are some stones for my slingshot."

So David went to a little creek that was nearby and he found five smooth stones in the water. He put them in his shepherd's bag and threw it over his shoulder. Then he took his slingshot and walked out into the valley where the giant Goliath was waiting.

Well, Goliath couldn't believe it when he saw how small and young David was. He'd been waiting for days for the Israelis to send out a big soldier to fight him. And now here came this boy, with no weapons that Goliath could see. So he screamed, "Am I a dog that you send out this boy to fight me?" And then he looked at David. "Come here," he said. "Let's get this over with fast."

But David shouted back, so that everybody could hear, both the Philistines and the soldiers of Israel, "You come to me with a sword and a spear. But I come to you in the name of God. Today God is with me. He will help me kill you. Then everybody will know that God is on the side of Israel."

Well, this made Goliath very angry. He came closer and closer, every giant step making a loud noise. But David just stood there with his five stones and his slingshot until Goliath was almost on top of him. Then David put one of those stones in his slingshot and he whirled it over his head—whoosh, whoosh, whoosh. And just as Goliath was ready to reach out and kill David with his sword, that stone hit Goliath— SMACK!—right in the middle of the forehead. Do you know what happened then? Goliath fell dead with a giant thud. The ground shook all around. All the soldiers on both hills could feel it. Then David took the giant's sword—and cut off Goliath's head!

The Philistines couldn't believe their eyes. This young boy had beaten their toughest soldier. Now *they* were afraid. They knew that God must be with David and with Israel. So they turned and ran. And the soldiers of Israel gave a shout of triumph. They remembered to give thanks to God and then they went running across the valley after the Philistines and chased them for miles and miles and miles.

David took the head of Goliath and brought it to the king. Now David was a hero. The king wanted him to marry his daughter. And many years later, after the king had died, the people of Israel made David their new king. And with the help of God, David took care of his people just as he had once taken care of his father's sheep.

DANIEL AND THE LIONS

Have you ever heard of a fellow named Daniel? He was a very, very great man. His story is in the Bible. It's one of my favorite stories, and I think you'll like it too.

Now, Daniel lived at a time when his people—the people of Israel—had been captured by the Babylonians. The king of Babylon was a man named Darius. Darius was a pretty good king and he ruled over a very large kingdom. His kingdom was so big, in fact, that he needed a lot of help running it. And one of the people whom he chose to help him was Daniel.

Darius picked Daniel because he knew Daniel was a very smart man and a very good man. Darius didn't care that Daniel wasn't a Babylonian, and he made Daniel one of his most important assistants—sort of a vice-president.

Well, this made some of the people of Babylon—some of the king's other assistants—very jealous. And they began to think of a way to get rid of Daniel. They knew how much Daniel loved God and how often he prayed to Him. And so they came to see the king and said, "King Darius, what a great and wise ruler you are. How lucky we are to have you for our king. Why, you are so great and wise that you are almost a god yourself. And so we think, Your Majesty, that for the next thirty days nobody should pray to any god or ask anything of any god. If somebody wants anything, he should come to you. And ask you. Because you are our god."

Darius liked hearing this. Can you imagine? But he did. And so he said, "All right. That's not a bad idea. I'm going to do what you suggest. I'm going to make it a rule that everybody has to ask me for whatever they want. And they can't pray to any god. If they do, they'll be put to death."

The king's order went out right away. But Daniel knew he could not obey it. He was a good assistant to King Darius. But, more than that, Daniel was a good servant of God. And he was not about to stop praying to God just because the king told him to. So every day Daniel went home and prayed to God. And he gave thanks to God. He did that three times a day just like he always had.

The king's other assistants hid outside Daniel's house. They weren't at all surprised to see him praying. Oh, no. They knew that's what Daniel would do. And they went rushing back to the king and said, "We have just come from Daniel's house. And guess what? He was praying! He prays three times a day to his God, the God of Israel. Now remember what you said, Your Majesty. You said that anyone who prayed to any god but you was going to be killed."

King Darius was very unhappy. He loved Daniel. He didn't want to hurt Daniel. But he *had* made that rule. He *had* signed his name to it. So what choice did he have?

When Daniel was brought before him, King Darius said, "Daniel, I'm sorry. I don't want to do this. But you did not obey my order. You prayed to your God. So you must be killed. I hope now that your God will hear you and save you, because I must put you in a cave with hungry lions." Then the king's soldiers came and put Daniel into the cave with all the lions.

That night King Darius didn't sleep at all. He was so worried about poor Daniel. And early the next morning he went running out to the lions' cave and he called out, "Oh, Daniel, was your God—the God you prayed to three times a day—able to save you from the lions?"

And right away King Darius heard a strong voice from inside the cave say, "Yes, Your Majesty, I'm fine. God *did* save me!"

It was Daniel! He was alive! King Darius couldn't believe it.

"Do you know that these lions never touched me, not once all night long!" Daniel shouted out to the king. "Angels of God kept the lions' mouths closed so they couldn't hurt me."

The king was so happy. He had Daniel taken out of the lions' cave and, sure enough, there wasn't even a scratch on him. Then King Darius knew that Daniel's God was the one real true God. And he also knew he had been tricked by those other assistants. So can you guess what King Darius did next? He had all those wicked assistants put in the lions' cave. Yes he did! The lions were even hungrier now because they hadn't gotten to eat Daniel. So now they had a fine big lunch!

And as for Daniel, well, King Darius made him an even more powerful assistant than he had been before. And Daniel helped the king rule over all the people in Babylon.

It's good to do what God says, isn't it? And it's good to pray to him every day, because then God blesses us and keeps us safe—just like He kept Daniel safe from all those hungry lions!

JONAH AND THE WHALE

Now I'm going to tell you a fish story. As you get older you'll probably hear lots of fish stories. Stories about big fish that people say they've caught. And if you hear them tell the story more than once, you may find that the fish grows a little bit bigger every time.

But this story isn't about a man who caught a fish. No. This story is about a fish that caught a man! And it's a true story. It's right in the Bible.

Once there was a man named Jonah. Jonah loved God and God loved Jonah. Sometimes God asked Jonah to do things for Him, and Jonah usually did what God asked. But one time God asked Jonah to do something that Jonah didn't want to do. No, he didn't want to do it one bit.

Here's what it was. God wanted him to go to a big city called Nineveh and tell everybody there, from the king on down, that God was going to destroy the city. God was going to burn it to the ground because all the people of Ninevah were so bad. Well, you can understand why Jonah didn't want to spread all that bad news. So instead of going to Nineveh, Jonah decided to run away.

But do you think anybody can really run away from God? No. You're right. Because God is everywhere. And He always knows what we're doing whether it's good or bad. But Jonah tried anyway. He got on a ship to sail to another country. But, do you know, a storm blew up while Jonah was at sea. It was a terrible storm, and it looked like any minute the ship was going to sink.

Of course, Jonah knew what the problem was. He knew that God had made that storm. God was punishing him because Jonah was not doing what God had asked.

So Jonah told the captains of the ship, "You'd better throw me overboard. Because if you do, the storm will stop and you'll be saved. But if you keep me, the ship is sure to sink."

And so the captain and his crew threw Jonah overboard into the raging storm in the middle of the ocean. Can you imagine that!

Jonah sank beneath the waves. But he didn't drown. Do you know what happened? A giant fish was in the water—God had put that fish there—and just as Jonah was sinking deeper and deeper, this great big fish came by and swallowed him. GULP!

Now, maybe you think Jonah died after that fish ate him. But no. Way down deep inside of that fish, way down in its belly, Jonah was still alive. For three days and three nights Jonah stayed inside the belly of that big fish.

And can you guess what he did all that time? He prayed. Wouldn't you pray if you were in Jonah's place way down inside a big smelly fish, out in the ocean? Boy, I know I would. Jonah said, "God, you were always so good to me. I'm sorry I didn't do what you asked. I know that if you didn't love me, I would have drowned when I fell into the ocean. But instead you had this big fish swallow me up. So I believe that you'll give me another chance to do what you wanted."

Then Jonah thanked God, because even though God hadn't given him another chance yet, Jonah was just sure he would. And do you know, a very strange thing happened then. The fish hiccuped! He went "HICCUP!" and out came Jonah.

Jonah swam ashore, and you'll never guess in a million years where he was. Right outside the city of Nineveh, right where God had wanted him to go in the first place! The fish had been swimming toward Nineveh the whole time Jonah was inside its belly!

Well, Jonah went inside the city and he began shouting in the street. "All you people of Nineveh have been very wicked!" Jonah shouted. "So now you'd better leave this city because in forty days God is going to destroy it."

Jonah was sure everybody would laugh at him and chase him away. But they didn't. All the people of Nineveh believed him. Somehow they knew that what Jonah was saying was true. They knew they were hearing the word of God. And they were all sorry that they had been so bad. Even the king. He took off his royal robes and put on rags and he prayed along with all the other people. "Oh, God, please forgive us!" they all cried. "Please give us another chance and don't destroy our city."

God heard their prayers and He decided that, yes, He would give the people of Nineveh a second chance. Just like He had given Jonah a second chance. So He didn't destroy the city and everybody lived very happily for many years, doing what God wanted them to do.

Now, that's a nice way for a story to end, don't you think?

And you know what else?

When you are bigger, you'll be able to read the Bible all by yourself. Yes, you will. You can read the story of Jonah, and David, and Noah, as well as many other wonderful stories that aren't in this book, just as they were first written, so very, very long ago.